My Kingdom for a Horse

AN ANTHOLOGY OF POEMS ABOUT HORSES

EDITED BY

Betty Ann Schwartz

ILLUSTRATED BY

Alix Berenzy

HENRY HOLT AND COMPANY

NEW YORK

To Philip
and to all the poets who contributed
to this collection —B. A. S.

For Daniel and Ray —A. B.

Henry Holt and Company, LLC, *Publishers since 1866*
115 West 18th Street, New York, New York 10011
Henry Holt is a registered trademark of Henry Holt and Company, LLC
Compilation copyright © 2001 by Betty Ann Schwartz
Illustrations copyright © 2001 by Alix Berenzy
All rights reserved.
Published in Canada by Fitzhenry & Whiteside Ltd.,
195 Allstate Parkway, Markham, Ontario L3R 4T8.
Library of Congress Cataloging-in-Publication Data
My kingdom for a horse: an anthology of poems about horses/
[selected by] Betty Ann Schwartz; illustrated by Alix Berenzy.   p.   cm.
1. Horses—Juvenile poetry. 2. Children's poetry, American.
[1. Horses—Poetry. 2. American poetry.] I. Schwartz, Betty Ann.
II. Berenzy, Alix, ill. III. Title.
PS595.H67M9 2001 811.008'036296655—dc21 00-40976
ISBN 0-8050-6212-2 / First Edition—2001 / Designed by Donna Mark
The artist used pastels and graphite pencils on Pastel Delux handmade
paper to create the illustrations for this book.
Printed in the United States of America on acid-free paper. ∞

10 9 8 7 6 5 4 3 2 1

Permission to use the following is gratefully acknowledged:

Pages 8–9: "Night Clouds," from *The Complete Poetical Works of Amy Lowell.* Copyright © 1955 by Houghton Mifflin Co. Copyright © renewed 1983 by Houghton Mifflin Co., Brinton P. Roberts, and G. D'Andelot Belin, Esq. Reprinted by permission of Houghton Mifflin Co. All rights reserved.

Page 10: "The Unicorn," reprinted by permission of Sterling Lord Literistic, Inc. Copyright 1957 by William Smith.

Page 12: "Early One Morning on Featherbed Lane," from *Ride a Purple Pelican,* by Jack Prelutsky. Copyright © 1986 by Jack Prelutsky. Reprinted by permission of Greenwillow Books, a division of William Morrow & Company, Inc.

Page 13: "In the Beauty Parlor," by April Halprin Wayland. Printed by permission of the author.

Page 15: "Merry-Go-Round," from *Good Morning, Last Poems,* by Mark Van Doren. Copyright © 1973 by the Estate of Mark Van Doren. Reprinted by permission of Hill and Wang, a division of Farrar, Straus & Giroux, Inc.

Page 16: "Equestrienne," by Rachel Field. Reprinted with the permission of Simon & Schuster Books for Young Readers, an imprint of Simon & Schuster Children's Publishing Division, from *Branches Green,* by Rachel Field. Copyright 1934 Macmillan Publishing Company; copyright renewed © 1962 Arthur S. Pederson.

Page 18: "My Pony," by Ruth Feder. Printed by permission of the author.

Page 19: "Giddy Up," by James Minor. Printed by permission of the author.

Page 21: "A Pony," copyright © 1971 Aileen Fisher. Copyright © renewed 1999 by Aileen Fisher. Used by permission of Marian Reiner for the author.

Page 22: "Tommy," by Tony Johnston. Printed by permission of the author.

Page 23: "The Policeman's Horse," by Betty Ann Schwartz. Printed by permission of the author.

Page 24: "The Filly at the Qualifying Race," by Kristine O'Connell George. Printed by permission of the author.

Page 27: "Retired to Pasture," copyright © 2001 by Anita Wintz. Used by permission of Marian Reiner for the author.

Page 28: "The Runaway," from *The Poetry of Robert Frost,* edited by Edward Connery Lathem. Copyright 1923, © 1969 by Henry Holt and Company; copyright 1951 by Robert Frost. Reprinted by permission of Henry Holt and Company, LLC.

Page 30: "Foal," copyright Estate of Mary Britton Miller.

Page 31: "Stable at Daybreak," copyright © 2001 by Anita Wintz. Used by permission of Marian Reiner for the author.

Page 32: "White Horse by Moonlight," by Tony Johnston. Printed by permission of the author.

Page 34: "Moondrop," by Joan Bransfield Graham. Printed by permission of the author.

Page 35: "The Horseman," by Walter de la Mare, reprinted by permission of The Literary Trustees of Walter de la Mare and the Society of Authors as their representative.

Page 40: "My Horse, Fly Like a Bird," copyright © 1989 by Virginia Driving Hawk Sneve. All rights reserved. Reprinted from *Dancing Teepees: Poems of American Indian Youth,* by permission of Holiday House, Inc.

Contents

Night Clouds

The white mares of the moon rush along the sky
Beating their golden hoofs upon the glass Heavens;
The white mares of the moon are all standing on their hind legs
Pawing at the green porcelain doors of the remote Heavens.

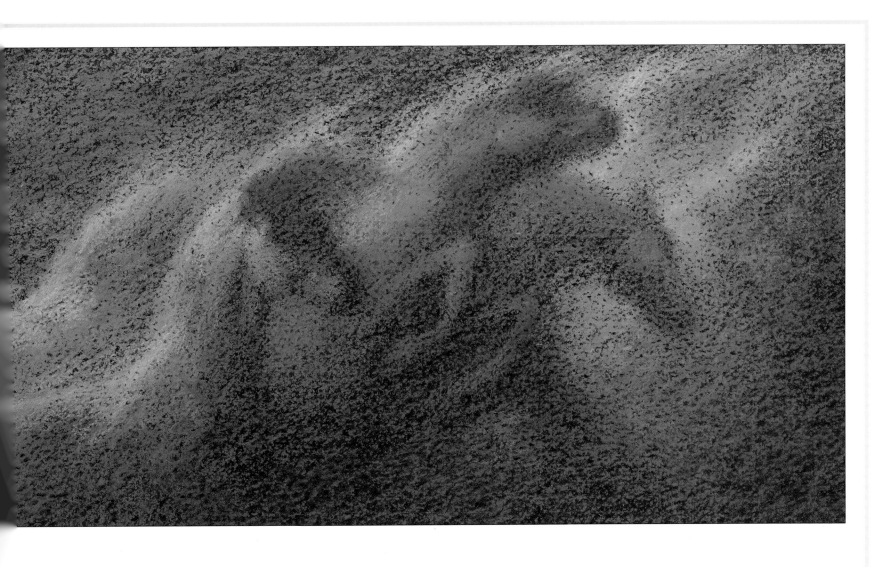

Fly, Mares!
Strain your utmost,
Scatter the milky dust of stars,
Or the tiger sun will leap upon you and destroy you
With one lick of his vermilion tongue.

—Amy Lowell

The Unicorn

The Unicorn with the long white horn
    Is beautiful and wild.
He gallops across the forest green
So quickly that he's seldom seen
Where Peacocks their blue feathers preen
    And strawberries grow wild.
He flees the hunter and the hounds,
Upon black earth his white hoof pounds,
Over cold mountain streams he bounds
    And comes to a meadow mild;
There, when he kneels to take his nap,
He lays his head in a lady's lap
    As gently as a child.

—*William Jay Smith*

Early One Morning on Featherbed Lane

Early one morning on Featherbed Lane,
I saw a white horse with a strawberry mane,
I jumped on his back just as fast as I could,
and we galloped away to the green willow wood.

We galloped all morning with never a stop,
where mockingbirds whistle and ladybugs hop,
we drank from a stream where the water runs free,
and we slept in the shade of a green willow tree.

—*Jack Prelutsky*

In the Beauty Parlor

I am sitting under the chair
the haircutting lady is trimming Mom's hair.
My horse is asking, "Is there any more?"
grazing in curls upon the floor.

—*April Halprin Wayland*

Merry~Go~Round

Horses in front of me,
Horses behind,
But mine is the best one,
He never looks down.
He rises and falls
As if there were waves,
But he never goes under,
Oh, music, oh, mine.

He is steady and strong,
And he knows I am here,
He says he is glad
That I picked him to ride.
But he hasn't a name.
I told him my own,
And he only went faster,
Oh, music, oh, mine.

Around and around,
And the people out there
Don't notice how happy
I am, I am.
The others are too,
But I am the most,
The most, the most,
Oh, music, oh, mine.

—*Mark Van Doren*

15

Equestrienne

See, they are clearing the sawdust course
For the girl in pink on the milk-white horse.
Her spangles twinkle; his pale flanks shine,
Every hair of his tail is fine
And bright as a comet's; his mane blows free
And she points a toe and bends a knee,
The while his hoofbeats fall like rain
Over and over and over again.
And nothing that moves on land or sea
Will seem so beautiful to me
As the girl in pink on the milk-white horse
Cantering over the sawdust course.

—*Rachel Field*

My Pony

The leaves
are crisp,
the morning
pure.
My pony's
hooves
are quick
and sure.
So early yet
that birds
still nest.
So dark,
as yet,
the farmers rest.
No saddle,
bridle, bit
for me,
I grip my
pony's mane,
and we
are one,
together,
galloping
free.

—*Ruth Feder*

Giddy Up

gid   dy
up   gid
dy   up
gid   dy   up
gid   dy   up
gid   dy   up
giddy   up
giddy up   giddy up
giddyup   giddyup
giddyupgiddyupgiddyup
giddyupgiddyupgiddyup

—James Minor

A Pony

Wish I had a pony
who would nuzzle, nuzzle, nuzzle
with his silky-satin muzzle.

Wish I had a pony
I could straddle, straddle, straddle,
so I wouldn't need a saddle.

Wish I had a white one,
a just-the-proper-height one.

Wish I had a red one,
a star-upon-his-head one.

Wish I had a brown one,
a trotting-up-and-down one.

Wish I had a pony
with a name like Tuck or Tony
who was plump instead of bony
(though a bony one would do) . . .

Wish it didn't take so long
for wishes to come true.

—*Aileen Fisher*

Tommy

Come down from your hill
                of grass
where you spend your old
age
                      cropping,
grazing on
summer days.

Come down from your secret
place.
I'll turn my back
and never know
where you most love
                to go.

When you reach the gate
(that you've rubbed to glass),
whinny
                for me.
I'll hear, no matter what.
And I'll come out
and feed you your favorite
                    treat,
golden as your coat—
pancakes.

—Tony Johnston

The Policeman's Horse

Standing tall
Gentle and brave
A marvel of poise
Despite the city's incessant noise

Do I dare approach
And touch his nose?

—Betty Ann Schwartz

The Filly at the Qualifying Race

She's thunder, drumming down a dirt track.
She's wind, flowing muscle, pounding fast.
She's storm, fierce, wide-eyed raging past
the other straining horses, until, at last,
the filly sees her chance, that narrow gap—

Her trainer leans hard against the rail—
she's a blur of wind-whipped mane and tail.
She's crack of lightning bolting through.
He smiles, nods and says, "She'll do."

—*Kristine O'Connell George*

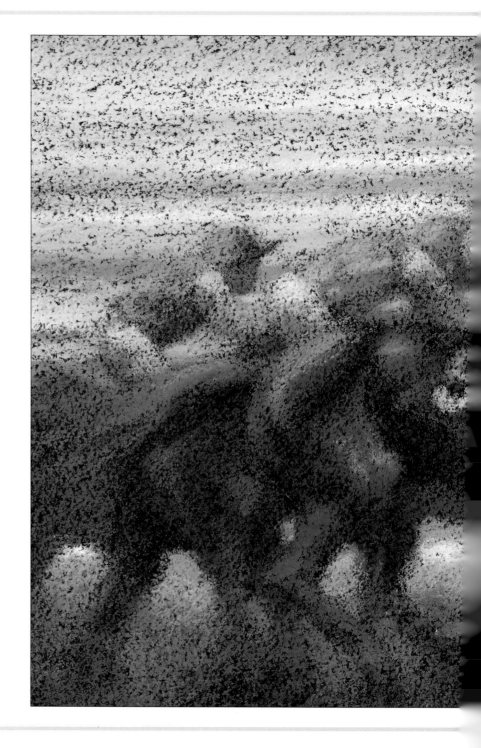

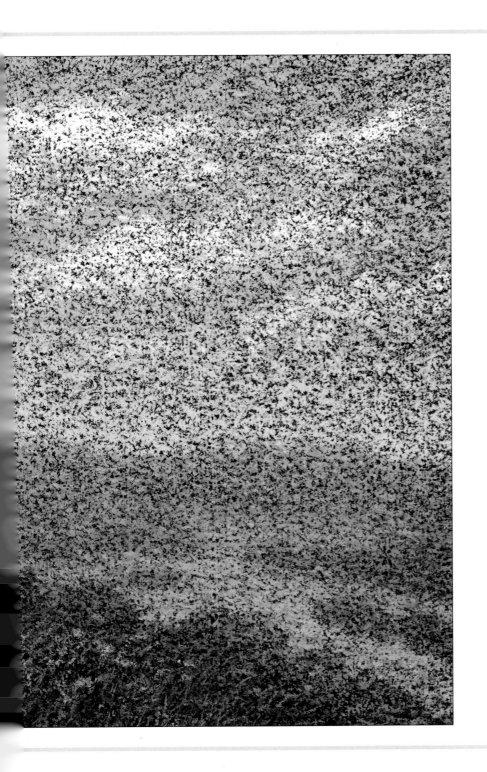

Retired to Pasture

The meadow moist with morning dew
Is calling me to canter through
Its oak lined paths of pasture grass.
The brook beside it, as I pass,
Invites me down to quench my thirst.
To think that I had once been cursed
To trot upon the city streets
With honking cars in sweltering heat!
Refreshed am I as wind blown wheat.

—*Anita Wintz*

The Runaway

Once when the snow of the year was beginning to fall,
We stopped by a mountain pasture to say, "Whose colt?"
A little Morgan had one forefoot on the wall,
The other curled at his breast. He dipped his head
And snorted at us. And then he had to bolt.
We heard the miniature thunder where he fled,
And we saw him, or thought we saw him, dim and gray,
Like a shadow against the curtain of falling flakes.
"I think the little fellow's afraid of the snow.
He isn't winter-broken. It isn't play
With the little fellow at all. He's running away.
I doubt if even his mother could tell him, 'Sakes,
It's only weather.' He'd think she didn't know!
Where is his mother? He can't be out alone."
And now he comes again with clatter of stone,
And mounts the wall again with whited eyes
And all his tail that isn't hair up straight.
He shudders his coat as if to throw off flies.
"Whoever it is that leaves him out so late,
When other creatures have gone to stall and bin,
Ought to be told to come and take him in."

—Robert Frost

Foal

Come trotting up
Beside your mother,
Little skinny.

Lay your neck across
Her back, and whinny,
Little foal.

You think you're a horse
Because you can trot—
But you're not.

Your eyes are so wild,
And each leg is as tall
As a pole;

And you're only a skittish
Child, after all,
Little foal.

—*Mary Britton Miller*

Stable at Daybreak

To touch a rippling
nose of damp velvet,
to see warm breath
rise in wisps of smoke
misting morning,
to hear vibrating lips
roll back releasing
a long leathery tongue
to take hold of so small
a cube of sugar—
is "horse."

—Anita Wintz

White Horse
by Moonlight

Santo feeds
while the moon
comes up
curved like the bowl
of a silver spoon,
buries his nose
in silver
weeds.
Santo
the color
of moon.

—*Tony Johnston*

Moondrop

Kathleen lies
on the picnic table
near the corral,
in the mist, under the moon.

Hours pass by—
since she cannot hear,
she watches the mare,
watches for her
to heave and twist,
to push her colt
into this world.

She must help to turn him—
all legs and urgent muscle,
warm breath and long
whiskers on the chin.

She brings her daughter
on sleep-wobbled legs
to see this vision
in the night—
to share it—
in the mist, under the moon.

—*Joan Bransfield Graham*

The Horseman

I heard a horseman
    Ride over the hill;
The moon shone clear,
The night was still;
His helm was silver,
    And pale was he;
And the horse he rode
    Was of ivory.

—*Walter de la Mare*

Horses

The horses of the sea
    Rear a foaming crest,
But the horses of the land
    Serve us the best.

The horses of the land
    Munch corn and clover,
While the foaming sea-horses
    Toss and turn over.

—Christina Rossetti

from The War God's Horse Song

I am the Turquoise Woman's son

On top of Belted Mountain beautiful horses
Slim like a weasel

My horse has a hoof like striped agate
His fetlock is like fine eagle plume
His legs are like quick lightning

My horse's body is like an eagle-feathered arrow

My horse has a tail like a trailing black cloud

I put flexible goods on my horse's back

The Holy Wind blows through his mane
His mane is made of rainbows

My horse's ears are made of round corn

My horse's eyes are made of stars

My horse's head is made of mixed waters
   (from the holy waters)
   (he never knows thirst)

My horse's teeth are made of white shell

The long rainbow is in his mouth for a bridle
With it I guide him

—*Navajo Indians, North America*

My Horse, Fly Like a Bird

My horse, fly like a bird
To carry me far
From the arrows of my enemies,
And I will tie red ribbons
To your streaming hair.

—*Virginia Driving Hawk Sneve*
(adapted from a Lakota warrior's song to his horse)

from Song of Myself

A gigantic beauty of a stallion, fresh and responsive to my caresses.
Head high in the forehead, wide between the ears,
Limbs glossy and supple, tail dusting the ground,
Eyes full of sparkling wickedness, ears finely cut, flexibly moving.
His nostrils dilate as my heels embrace him,
His well-built limbs tremble with pleasure as we race around
    and return.

—*Walt Whitman*

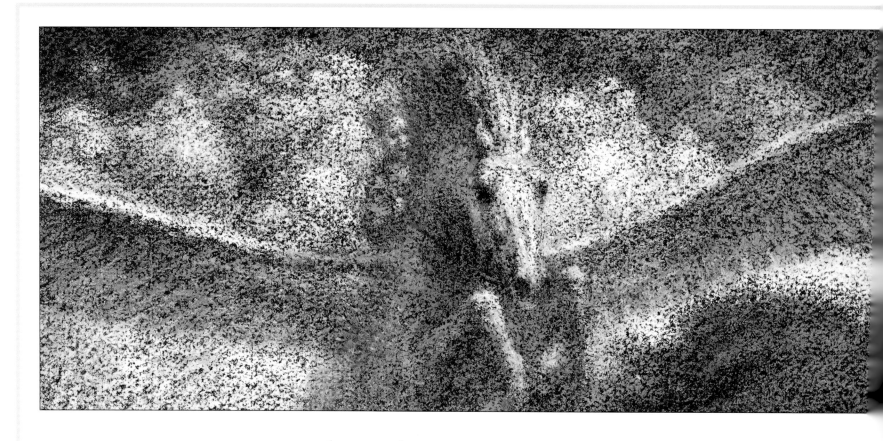

from The Fly-Away Horse

Oh, a wonderful horse is the Fly-Away Horse—
Perhaps you have seen him before;
Perhaps, while you slept, his shadow has swept
Through the moonlight that floats on the floor.
For it's only at night, when the stars twinkle bright,
That the Fly-Away Horse, with a neigh
And a pull at his rein and a toss of his mane,
Is up on his heels and away!

The Moon in the sky,
As he gallopeth by,
Cries: "Oh! what a marvellous sight!"
And the Stars in dismay
Hide their faces away
In the lap of old Grandmother Night.

—*Eugene Field*

The Horse

I will not change my horse with any that treads.

When I bestride him, I soar, I am a hawk.

He trots the air. The earth sings when he touches it.

The basest horn of his hoof is more musical than the pipe of Hermes . . .

He's of the color of the nutmeg.

And of the heat of the ginger.

He is pure air and fire; and the dull elements of earth and water
    never appear in him,

But only in patient stillness while his rider mounts him.

It is the prince of palfreys.

His neigh is like the bidding of a monarch,

And his countenance enforces homage.

—William Shakespeare
(from *Henry V*, act 3, scene 7)

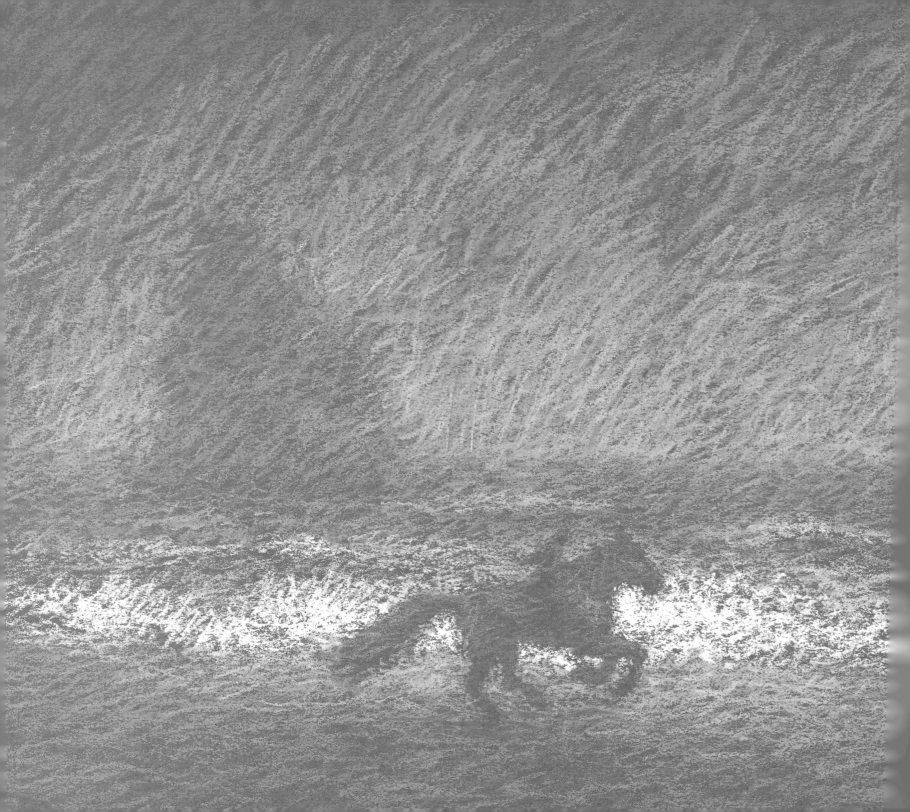